CONTENTS

WHAT IS FOOTBALL?

Association football, also known as soccer, features two teams, each with 11 players. These players move a ball around a pitch using their feet, heads, chests and legs – only the goalkeepers can use their hands or arms.

HOW LONG IS A MATCH?

A full game of football lasts 90 minutes. This is split into two equal halves, each lasting 45 minutes. In some competitions, such as the World Cup, periods of extra time are played if the scores are level after the full 90 minutes. Matches for younger players often last for shorter periods and they may feature fewer players.

GOALS

A football team aims to keep possession of the ball and score goals, while stopping the other team scoring goals. A goal is scored when the ball crosses the goal line between the goal posts and underneath the goal's crossbar. The team with the most goals at the end of the game wins.

A substitution sees one player leave the field to be replaced by a new player. Coaches substitute players because of tiredness or injury, or when they want to bring on a different type of player. For example, they may wish to play an extra attacker and take off a defender.

crossbar   goalkeeper

goal post

WHITEKNIGHTS
11

A goalkeeper gets ready to make a save from an attacking player. Goalkeepers are the only players allowed to handle the ball and, then, only when they are inside their own penalty areas (see pages 22–23).

SPORTING SKILLS

FOOTBALL

CLIVE GIFFORD

WAYLAND

First published in 2008 by Wayland

Reprinted 2008

Copyright © Wayland 2008

Wayland
Hachette Children's Books
338 Euston Road
London NW1 3BH

Wayland Australia
Level 17/207 Kent Street
Sydney, NSW 2000

Managing Editor: Rasha Elsaeed
Produced by Tall Tree Ltd
Editor: Jon Richards
Designer: Ben Ruocco
Photographer: Michael Wicks
Consultant: Steve Pearse

British Library Cataloguing in Publication Data

Gifford, Clive
    Football. - (Sporting skills)
    1. Soccer - Juvenile literature
    I. Title
    796.3'34

ISBN 9780750253772

Printed in China

Wayland is a division of Hachette Children's Books, an Hachette Livre UK company.

Picture credits
All photographs taken by Michael Wicks, except:
Cover Dreamstime.com/Dragan Trifunovic,
5 Magi Hardoun/epa/Corbis

Acknowledgements
The author and publisher would like to thank the following people for their help and participation in this book:
Whiteknights FC and Paul Scholey

The website addresses (URLs) included in this book were valid at the time of going to press. However, because of the nature of the Internet, it is possible that some addresses may have changed, or sites may have changed or closed down since publication. While the author and Publisher regret any inconvenience this may cause the readers, no responsibility for any such changes can be accepted by either the author or the Publisher.

Disclaimer
In preparation of this book, all due care has been exercised with regard to the advice, activities and techniques depicted. The publishers regret that they can accept no liability for any loss or injury sustained. When learning a new sport it is important to get expert tuition and to follow a manufacturer's instructions.

Pitch positions

A team organises itself with one goalkeeper and lines of defenders, midfielders and attackers. The numbers of each type of player are used to describe the formation. For example, '4-4-2' means that there are four defenders, four midfielders and two attackers. Coaches will choose different formations to suit the type of game they want to play. A defensive formation could have five defenders and only one attacker – '5-4-1'.

Manchester United and Portugal attacker, Cristiano Ronaldo blasts a shot towards the goal.

THE PITCH AND PLAY

Football is played on a large grass or artificial pitch. The precise size of a pitch can vary, but the markings on every full pitch are the same. These include a large box known as the penalty area and a smaller box inside that, called the goal area. The four corners of a pitch are marked with corner flags.

The pitch

A football pitch is split into two halves by the halfway line, with a centre spot and centre circle in the middle. The game is started with a kick-off taken from the centre spot, with all players in their own half of the pitch. A kick-off is also used to restart the game after a goal has been scored.

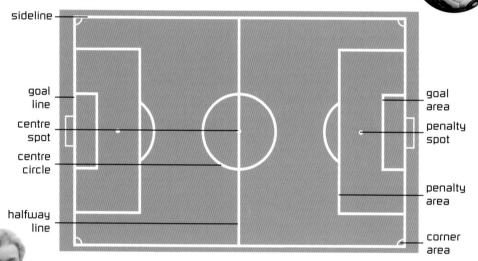

sideline

goal line

centre spot

centre circle

halfway line

goal area

penalty spot

penalty area

corner area

IN AND OUT OF PLAY

The whole of the ball has to cross a sideline or goal line for the ball to be out of play. If a ball goes out of play over a sideline, then a throw-in is awarded (see page 7). If a defender is the last player to touch the ball when it goes over the goal line, then a corner is awarded to the attacking team. The corner is taken from the small area beside the corner flag.

This player is running up the edge of the pitch with the ball under control. If she kicks the ball so that it curves out past the sideline in the air but lands inside the pitch, the ball is still said to have gone out of play and a throw-in will be awarded (see page 7).

1 When the ball goes out over the sidelines, the officials will signal a throw-in. The player takes a throw-in from where the ball went out and must stand with both feet on or behind the sideline.

2 The player takes the ball back behind his or her head with both hands and then brings it forwards, with both hands still on the ball. If he or she fails to do this or steps over the sideline, a foul throw is signalled and the other team is awarded the throw-in.

3 The player releases the ball with his or her hands following through towards the target. The player aims to get back onto the pitch as quickly as possible and so get back into the game.

THE OFFICIALS

A football match is controlled by a referee and two assistants, both of whom run along the sidelines. These officials decide when the ball is in or out of play, whether a goal has been scored and whether one of the game's laws has been broken. The referee uses a whistle to stop the game and has a range of signals to show his decisions to the players and spectators.

When a player performs a bad foul, the referee can award a yellow card. A second yellow card in a game or a red card for dangerous play sees the player leave the field. His or her team then plays on with one less player.

When the ball rolls over a defending team's goal line and the last player to touch it was an attacker, the referee and his assistants will signal for a goal kick. The goalkeeper or one of his team-mates places the ball inside the goal area and kicks it into play.

TRAINING AND KIT

Football is a very athletic sport and players need to be fit in order to compete successfully for an entire match. Training hard, warming up and wearing the proper kit will also give a player the best chance of success.

FOOTBALL KIT

A player's football kit is relatively straightforward, but there are important details worth paying attention to. The clothing you wear should be comfortable and not restrict your movement. Jewellery and watches are not allowed to be worn. You should also wear a tracksuit to keep you warm after a match or a training session.

Football shirts are lightweight and should be a comfortable fit. They have either long sleeves (shown here) or short sleeves.

Tucking the shirt into your shorts is not just a matter of looking neat. It also gives a defender less chance to pull your shirt and hold you back.

Football shorts are usually elasticated at the waist and have a drawstring to keep them up.

Types of boots

Football boots come with different sole types for different conditions. Here is an astro boot for playing on artificial pitches (top), a grass pitch boot with wedges called blades to provide grip (middle), and finally a boot with round studs, which is also used on grass (bottom).

Long football socks are kept up using a sock garter, tape or a ring of elastic.

Shinpads protect the bony front part of your lower leg from painful knocks.

Football boots should fit your foot really well and offer support around your ankle. Good boots are made of soft leather so that you can feel the ball during play.

The shin pads are held in place underneath the socks usually by a couple of fastening strips.

Whatever type of boot you wear, make sure that the laces are tied securely and do not dangle to the ground where they could trip you up.

WARMING UP

Before any training session or match, you should always warm-up and stretch. Warming-up can involve a mixture of jogging, skipping and other exercises. These help to get blood flowing around your body freely to prepare you for the hard work ahead. After a warming-up period, you should stretch the key muscles in your upper and lower legs, your groin and your back, shoulders and arms. Stretches are performed gently and repeated, and help prevent injury. Ask your coach to show you how to perform a range of stretches.

Stretching

These players are stretching the muscles at the backs of their legs. They are following instructions from their coach as they ease gently into the stretch and hold the position.

PRACTICE MAKES PERFECT

Training and practice are the keys to football success. Training will improve sharpness and reactions and improve your passing, heading, shooting and defending. It also gets you working with others as a team and improves your fitness so that you can perform at your best throughout a long game.

You will sweat a lot during a long training session or a full game of football. Players top up the fluids they have lost by taking small sips of water during breaks in training or at half-time.

These four players are involved in a '2 v 2' drill in a small area marked out with cones. One pair of players tries to keep control of the ball and pass it to a team-mate, while the opposing pair tries to intercept the ball. Training drills like these help to improve your game.

PASSING THE BALL

Passing moves the ball from one player to another and good passing between team-mates can get the ball into attacking positions quickly. Passing should be practised as often as possible, and players should work especially hard with their weaker feet so that they can pass using both their left and right feet.

TYPES OF PASSING

There are a number of ways the ball can be passed. Players can use their heads or chests to deflect balls to team-mates. However, most passes are made using the feet and they can vary in their distance, height and speed.

When making short, accurate passes, players tend to hit through the middle of the ball so that they keep it close to the ground. For more height on a pass, players lean back a little as they make the pass and aim to hit through the lower part of the ball, lifting it off the ground.

sidefoot

outside   instep

These are the three main areas of the boot that are used to make passes; the sidefoot, the instep where the laces of the boot are, and the outside of the foot.

Sidefoot pass

1 The sidefoot or push pass is the most common pass in football and the most accurate over shorter distances. The passer places his non-kicking foot beside the ball and gets his body over the ball. His head is up and he is looking at his target as he takes his foot back.

2 The kicking foot is swung forwards through the middle of the ball. The aim is to stroke the ball smoothly so that it skims along the surface of the grass to the receiver. The foot should follow through to point at the target.

1 The instep drive is used for long-distance passing as it can be made with much more force than the sidefoot pass. The player plants his non-kicking foot by the side of the ball and takes his kicking leg back.

2 With his arms out to help balance and his body over the ball, the player's kicking leg swings forwards with the toes pointing down. The aim is for the instep to connect with the middle of the ball.

3 The kicking foot drives through the ball, with the ankle stretched down. The kicking foot follows through after the ball has left. Hitting the lower half of the ball with your body leaning slightly back will send the ball higher.

The outside of the boot can be used to make a flicked pass. The boot's toes swing outwards and away from the player's body to nudge or flick the ball to the side. Aim to connect with the middle of the ball to keep it low. This sort of pass can be used to send the ball 'round the corner' for a team-mate close by to run onto.

FORCE, TIMING AND ACCURACY

When making a pass, your thoughts should be on the team-mate you are passing to, who is known as the receiver. Your pass should reach the receiver so that the ball is easy to control. A pass hit with too much or not enough force is unlikely to be successful. Timing and accuracy are vital as well. When your receiver is on the move, you have to time the exact moment you make a pass and aim it to travel to a point ahead of the receiver. That way, he or she will reach the ball and collect it without having to slow down or stop running.

Backheels

The backheel pass is used to pass the ball to a player behind and so reverse the direction of play. The passer swings his foot forwards a short distance and then back towards the ball.

The player aims for the back of his heel to strike through the middle of the ball to send the ball backwards along the ground.

RECEIVING THE BALL

How the passer hits the ball is not the end of the passing story. If a well-hit and accurate pass is not controlled by the receiver, then the whole pass fails and the opposing team may get possession. Receiving the ball well calls for awareness of the game around you, an excellent first touch and good cushioning skills.

CUSHIONING THE BALL

The ball will often travel towards a receiver at high speed. Cushioning is the skill of slowing down, or 'killing', the ball's pace so that it is under control at the player's feet. It involves the player relaxing the part of the body about to hit the ball and moving this body part back as the ball connects with it. This helps to slow the ball down. The ball can be cushioned using your chest, thigh or various parts of the foot.

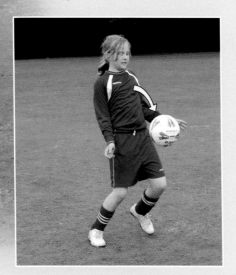

chest cushion

1 This player watches the ball as she leans back to perform a chest cushion. She keeps her arms out with her hands open so that her chest muscles are relaxed.

2 As the ball hits the player's chest, she relaxes and brings her arms and shoulders in to help slow the ball so that it rolls off her and drops downwards.

3 The ball drops to the player's feet ready for her to control and make her next move, such as a shot at goal, a pass or a run with the ball.

1 With her eye on the ball, this player bends her knee and raises her leg. Her arms are out a little to help with her balance.

2 She aims for the ball to land on the top of her thigh, which she relaxes and pulls back down to cushion the ball.

3 As the ball drops, so does her leg so that both feet are on the floor ready to control the ball.

HIGH AND WIDE

Choosing which part of your body to control a ball with depends on the speed and angle at which the ball is arriving. Players learn to control the ball in many different ways. A dropping high ball, for instance, can be taken and controlled on the top of the thigh or on the chest. A wide ball may need the player to stretch his or her leg out to get it under control using the top or side of the boot.

This player is using the inside of his foot to control the ball. He has turned his foot so that the inside is in line and faces the direction from where the ball is arriving. As the ball arrives, he brings his foot back to slow the ball down.

This player is cushioning the ball with the instep of the boot. The foot is taken back and down as the ball arrives.

YOUR NEXT MOVE

As you are cushioning the ball, your thoughts should be on the next move. Receiving the ball well means you can get passing, shooting or on the move and running with the ball as quickly as possible and so avoid being challenged by an opponent.

MOVEMENT IN PLAY

Moving with and without the ball is essential for a team to perform well in a football match. Players without the ball must know how to move into space to receive it. Players with the ball must be skilled at running with it, protecting it from opponents and, sometimes, they must be able to beat an opponent.

SHIELDING

When receiving the ball, you may not be able to move forwards because an opponent is very close to you. In this situation, you may try to shield the ball by getting your body between the ball and the opponent. When shielding, a player has to look for his or her next move. This may be a lay off (a pass backwards or to the side) or a sharp turn to beat the defender (see right).

OFF THE BALL

Moving into space often means getting free of a defender who is marking you (guarding you closely). A player trying to get free of a marker often uses a fake or dummy move where he or she drops one shoulder and leans in that shoulder's direction, but sprints away in another direction. Quick changes of pace and direction are other ways of getting free of defenders and into a position to receive the ball.

The player in blue cuts away sharply from an opponent. She sprints into space with the aim of receiving a pass from a team-mate.

Turning

1 The player in blue is shielding the ball. He turns and moves to get his body between the ball and the opponent.

2 The attacker makes his move, pushing the ball to one side and turning sharply while protecting the ball with his body.

3 Once the attacker has turned, he looks to sprint away quickly from the opponent.

14

BEATING OPPONENTS

In many situations, a series of quick passes helps to move the ball past opponents. Sometimes, though, a player may choose to go past an opponent on his or her own. This can be done by accelerating quickly or by dribbling. Dribbling is moving the ball forwards with a series of close nudges and taps. It can be very useful for beating defenders, especially if it is combined with dummying (see right).

1 A player dribbling the ball has already leaned to his left to suggest that he will be heading in that direction.

Dribbling

Good dribbling technique involves keeping your head up and looking around for your next move. The ball should never be too far in front of you and out of your control.

2 The defender is uncertain in which direction the dribbler intends to go and is flat-footed. The dribbler drives off his left foot to actually head to his right.

1 This attacker (in blue) has spotted a lot of space behind a defender. The attacker decides to try a push-and-go move.

2 He sidefoot passes the ball to one side of the defender carefully judging how much force to use.

3 He sprints quickly past his opponent on the other side to collect the ball behind the defender.

ATTACKING PLAY

Attacking is all about creating chances to score goals. When players receive the ball, they first look to get it away from their own penalty area and then to attack and get inside or close to their opponents' penalty area.

DID YOU KNOW?

In 2001, Australia recorded the biggest win in international football by beating American Samoa 31–0.

1 An overlap is where an attacker without the ball makes a run down the side of the pitch ahead of the player with the ball. The attacker on the far left makes his overlapping run so that he is not offside as the ball is played (see page 17).

Overlap

2 The pass is played behind the defenders in yellow for the overlapping player to run onto. If successful, he is likely to be in a superb position to cross or shoot.

In this one-two move, or wall pass move, the player (right) makes a sidefoot pass to a team-mate and then sprints forwards. The team-mate passes behind the defender so that the first player can run onto the ball, control it and move forward or take a shot.

TEAM ATTACKS

Pieces of individual skill, such as successful dribbling, can sometimes create a goal scoring chance. However, most chances are created through players working together as a team with quick passing and running to create space. Players can make runs which draw defenders to them, creating gaps for other team-mates to move into.

1 A 'through ball' is a pass made behind one or more defenders. The passer spots the run of his team-mate and has to time and direct his pass perfectly to match his team-mate's run.

2 The pass is threaded through a gap between the defenders. The receiver, timing her run so that she is not offside (see below), is now behind the defence with a clear run on goal.

Offside

Attackers have to be aware of the offside law – being caught offside will give the opposing team a free kick. A player is offside if, as the ball is played, he or she is nearer the other team's goal line than both the ball and the second-last opponent. A player is not offside if he or she is in their own half, receives the ball directly from a goal kick, corner or throw-in, or if he or she is level with the second-last opponent. The player shown below is nearer to the goal than the last defender as the ball is played. As a result, he is in an offside position.

OVERLOADS AND CROSSES

One key attacking tactic is to use the full width of the pitch to stretch the defence and obtain an overload – where there are more attackers than there are defenders. When the ball is in wide positions, it is often crossed. This is a pass made into the middle of the pitch, usually into the penalty area. Many crosses are hit high, aiming for the head of an attacker. However, when a team has made a fast break, a cross may be made along the ground for a team-mate to run onto and shoot.

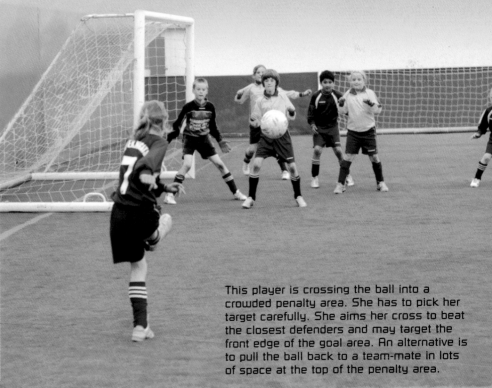

This player is crossing the ball into a crowded penalty area. She has to pick her target carefully. She aims her cross to beat the closest defenders and may target the front edge of the goal area. An alternative is to pull the ball back to a team-mate in lots of space at the top of the penalty area.

SHOOTING

Attacking counts for nothing unless goals are scored. This most often involves players taking shots on goal. Shots can come from all sorts of distances and angles, but they must be accurate and on target to be successful.

SHOT TYPES

Attackers close to goal may use a sidefoot pass as a shot to steer the ball away from the goalkeeper and any defenders. From longer distances, attackers often shoot using the instep drive (see page 11) which generates a lot more power than the sidefoot shot. Some players can bend or swerve the ball on long-distance shots (see right). This can confuse a goalkeeper or take the ball out of his or her reach and into the goal.

Swerving the ball

To bend the ball to the left, use the inside of your right boot to hit the right side of the ball and follow through straight.

To bend the ball to the right, kick through the left side of the ball with the outside of the right boot. Follow through across your body.

This attacker in blue is about to shoot from close range. With the keeper in the middle of the goal, the attacker can choose to aim at either corner.

SHOOTING SKILLS

Quick decision making, placement and good technique are all needed to turn shooting chances into goals. Opportunities come and go in an instant and players need to stay alert if they want to fire off a good shot. Quick reactions can also see a player get to a loose ball first to take a shot.

You may find shots sailing high or wide because you have stretched too far for the ball or have not got your body weight over it as you shoot. You should concentrate on making a clean contact through the middle of the ball and look to aim for a corner of the goal away from the goalkeeper.

Volleying

1 Volleying is striking the ball in mid-air. It can lead to a very powerful shot if performed well. This player keeps his eye on the ball as it travels towards him. He plans to make a front-on volley.

2 He lifts his shooting leg at the knee and takes his foot back a short distance. He points his toes down and keeps his arms out to help him balance.

3 As the ball drops, the player swings his leg through, keeping his toes pointed towards the ground. He times his swing so that his boot instep will meet the ball while the ball is still in the air.

4 The player's kicking leg follows through with a high knee lift. The player tries to keep his head over the ball as contact is made and the ball flies away. Leaning back is likely to result in the ball sailing away too high.

DID YOU KNOW?

Iran's Ali Daei has scored 109 goals in international matches, more than any other player.

FOLLOWING UP

Players should not relax and admire their shots. They must stay alert and follow up their attempts in case there is a deflection or block by a defender or keeper, or the ball hits the goal's crossbar or posts. Many goals are scored at the second attempt by alert attackers.

HEADING

Heading is a way of controlling the ball in the air. There is a range of different heading techniques that can be used for attacking, defending or passing to a team-mate.

HEADING TECHNIQUE

Many young players are scared of heading the ball, but heading does not hurt if you use the correct technique. This involves keeping your eyes on the ball until it hits your forehead – the ideal target area with which to head the ball. Start with gentle headers with your feet on the ground. Then you can build up power by arching your back a little and bringing your head forward to meet the ball, rather than just letting the ball hit your head.

Aim to connect using the centre of your forehead. Although your eyes are likely to shut on impact, try to keep them open as long as possible to watch the ball onto your head.

This player has jumped to get above the ball so that he can direct his attacking header downwards into the goal.

1 The player on the right makes a cushioned header, relaxing his neck and taking his head back as the ball arrives. He makes sure that his head is above the ball so the ball is directed downwards.

2 The cushioned header drops at the feet of a nearby team-mate. Sometimes, a player can make a cushioned header to bring a high ball down to the ground for him to control himself.

HEADING VARIATIONS

In a match, different types of header are used in different situations. A gentle header aimed to the side may be used by a defender to put the ball out of play or by an attacker to nod the ball on to a team-mate. Other headers are made with the player springing high in the air to get above an opponent or to get above the ball so that he or she can direct it downwards to a team-mate or into the goal. Diving headers, when players throw themselves at the ball, are the most spectacular of all headers. They are used only as a last resort when a player cannot reach the ball in any other way. Diving headers should be practised using a crash mat on the ground so as not to injure yourself.

This defender has made a strong defensive header. He has aimed to head powerfully through the lower half of the ball. This sends the ball up and forwards, clearing it out of danger.

GLANCES AND FLICK-ONS

The glancing header is used to deflect the ball to the side, such as when an attacker is in line with one goal post and wants to aim the ball for the other goal post. Flick-on headers are often made with the top of the forehead just brushing the ball to . send it over a defender and on to a team-mate.

As the ball is crossed in, this attacker has attempted a glancing header. He turns his head just before the ball arrives and uses the centre of his forehead to direct the ball towards the top corner of the goal.

GOALKEEPING

The primary role of a goalkeeper is to block shots on goal. However, good goalkeepers will also instruct defenders, command their penalty areas, stay aware and position themselves to stop opposition attacks early.

Low save

ALERT AND AWARE

Goalkeepers have an excellent view of a game, but they may not have to save a shot for many minutes. Concentrating on the game is very important, as they may have to rush off the goal line suddenly to stop attacks or to receive back passes from team-mates. If the ball is deliberately kicked back to them by a team-mate, they cannot pick it up but must instead kick or head it clear. As an opposition attack develops, keepers should get into the basic goalkeeping stance with their legs shoulder-width apart, their arms in front and bodyweight slightly forwards.

1 This keeper is in a good stance, knees bent slightly, springy on his feet and with his arms out. From this position he is able to move in any direction.

2 Moving from the ready position, the keeper bends the knee nearest to the direction he wants to dive and begins to push his legs away to drop his body down.

3 The keeper lands on his side to block the ball. He can either catch hold of the ball, or push it away with his hands.

This keeper has dropped to the ground on one knee. His body is behind the ball as it comes racing across the ground. He gets his hands under the ball and scoops it up into his chest.

BODY AS A BARRIER

Goalkeepers put in hours of practice saving shots from all different heights and angles. The vast majority of saves do not require spectacular diving. Instead, they rely on confident handling and good footwork to get into line with the ball's path. This way, the keeper's body acts as an extra barrier behind his or her hands.

To take a high ball, maximise the advantage you have over other players by stretching your arms up and catching the ball at the top of your jump. Try to take the ball slightly in front of you so that you can watch the ball into your hands.

Throwing the ball

Once the keeper has safely caught the ball, he can restart the game quickly by throwing it to a team-mate. Here, the keeper is using an underarm throw to roll the ball along the ground.

To get more distance on a throw, a keeper can use an overarm throw. This involves 'bowling' the ball with a straight arm in order to get the maximum distance.

CATCH, PUNCH OR DEFLECT

Catching the ball with both hands and gathering it into the body securely is the best option but, sometimes, the keeper is under pressure to reach the ball. If the keeper is uncertain about catching the ball securely, he or she may choose to punch the ball clear or deflect it with an open palm around the post or over the crossbar.

Using both fists together, this goalkeeper punches through the middle of the ball to send it flying out of danger.

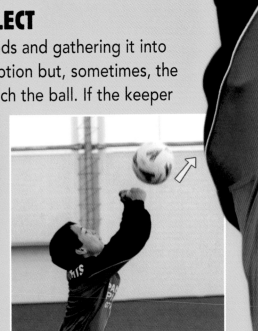

DEFENDING

A team without the ball has to defend and stop a goal being scored. Good defending requires great concentration and awareness from all players in the side. It involves a range of skills, such as marking and jockeying.

MARKING

Marking is the guarding of either an opponent (one-on-one) or an area of the pitch (zonal marking). One-on-one marking calls on all your powers of concentration to watch the opponent you are standing close to. The aim of one-on-one marking is to prevent your opponent from getting into enough space to receive the ball. When marking, try to stay goalside (closer to your goal than your opponent) at all times.

WORKING TOGETHER

All players in a side defend when they do not have the ball. At the back, defenders mark the opposing team's main attackers and move with them as they make runs. At the front, strikers and other attacking players chase down opponents with the ball trying to harass them into a mistake. Whatever position you play in, communicating with team-mates is vital for a strong defence, as is getting back into a good position if an attacker gets past you.

As the player in yellow tries to control the ball, the defender in blue sprints to close him down. By getting close to his opponent, the defending player cuts down the attacker's options to pass and run.

Defenders from the team in yellow each mark an attacker as the team in blue plans to take a corner. The defenders stay goalside of the players they are marking and try to follow their movements.

24

JOCKEYING

Jockeying involves getting close to an attacker with the ball and moving with him or her, always staying goalside, to try and slow down an attack. The aim is to try to delay the attacker until another team-mate arrives behind you. Then, you may be able to move in to make a tackle (see pages 26–27), or force the attacker away from the goal.

When facing a player with the ball, try to stay around 1 metre (3.5 feet) away, otherwise you may make it easy for them to get past you. Keep your eyes on the ball and try to slow the attacker down. Follow the movement of the ball and not the player. Standing slightly to one side can force your opponent to head in the opposite direction and away from your penalty area.

1 This defender in yellow has moved quickly to close down an attacker who has received the ball with his back to goal.

2 The defender gets up close behind the defender and tries to prevent him from turning without fouling him.

3 As the attacker moves, trying to find a way through, the defender also moves, taking the attacker away from the goal.

4 The delayed attacker has his foot on the ball to control it. However, the defender remains alert in case the attacker tries to perform a move to get past him.

TACKLING

When defending, there will be chances to try to regain the ball for your side by challenging an opponent for the ball. The most common technique used is the block tackle, which can be made from front-on or from the side. Other techniques include sliding and poke tackles.

1 The defender in yellow races towards an opponent who is dribbling with the ball. With the opponent not changing direction or passing, the defender decides to make a front block tackle.

2 As the defender gets close, he turns his tackling foot to present the whole inside of the foot towards the ball. He plants his non-tackling foot and bends the knee to provide himself with a firm base.

TACKLING TIPS

Good tackling relies on you being strong, balanced and decisive. Establishing a firm base with your supporting leg allows you to strike the ball with plenty of force, which will often wrestle it away from the control of your opponent. Timing your tackle is crucial. Lunging in too early or too late risks an opponent getting away from you or you committing a foul. Remember, the aim of challenging is not only to remove the ball from an opponent, but also to get the ball under your team's control. If your tackle sends the ball loose, look to get it under control as quickly as possible.

Front block

3 Keeping his body weight over the ball, he strikes it through the centre. The opponent loses control of the ball and the defender can take the ball away.

Side block tackle

The attacker in blue is running forwards but is not protecting the ball, which is on the defender's side. The defender in yellow plants his non-tackling leg and bends it at the knee. He hooks the inside of his other foot around the ball, dragging the ball away to safety.

Side tackle

1 The defender in yellow goes to make a sliding tackle from the side. He keeps his eyes on the ball as he bends his supporting leg – the leg nearest to his opponent when standing side to side.

2 Getting as low as possible, the tackler reaches across the opponent and hooks his foot around the ball. He must make contact with the ball rather than his opponent, otherwise he will give away a foul.

POKES AND NUDGES

In some match situations, a full-blooded tackle may not be possible or even necessary. For example, when tracking an opponent running along the sideline with the ball, stay alert in case he or she loses control of the ball or pushes it too far ahead. This can sometimes give you the chance to race across and move away with the ball. If that is not possible, you may be able to poke or nudge the ball out of his or her path with the toe of your boot.

3 The attacker loses possession of the ball. The tackler must get back onto his feet as quickly as possible to gain possession of the ball.

SET PIECES

When a football match is stopped by the referee's whistle or the ball goes out of play, it can be restarted in a number of ways. Kick-offs, goal kicks and throw-ins are three types of restart. The other three main restarts – corners, free kicks and penalties – are often known as set pieces.

CORNERS

A corner is awarded when a defender is the last player to touch the ball before it crosses the goal line. The corner is taken from the corner area nearest to where the ball went out of play. Attacking players will crowd the goal area, expecting a cross to come in that they can head into the goal. Alternatively, the corner taker may play a short pass to a team-mate who can cross from a different angle.

Corner taking

1 The corner taker can swing or bend the ball into or away from the goal. He may have made a signal to his team-mates beforehand so that they know where the ball is going.

2 Inside the penalty area, attackers and defenders will move, trying to get into a good position to either score a goal or clear the ball away from danger.

Free kick signals

Free kicks are awarded by a referee for a number of reasons, such as a player handling the ball or one player tripping an opponent. There are two types of free kick – direct and indirect. A direct free kick can be hit straight at goal while an indirect free kick has to be passed to a team-mate first. The opposing team must retreat 9 metres (10 yards) from where the free kick is being taken.

A direct free kick signal

An indirect free kick signal

FREE KICKS IN ATTACK

When a team is awarded a free kick inside the opponent's half, its thought must be to attack – but this does not necessarily mean a direct strike on goal. Free kicks from wide positions are often hit high into the penalty area. If a free kick is awarded in front of goal and within range of a shot, then the defending side may line up a number of players to form a wall in front of the goal. The challenge for the free kick taker is to bend the ball around or over the wall or to play a sideways pass to cut out the wall so that a team-mate can shoot.

Free kick

1 This player in blue lines up an attacking free kick. The defensive wall protects one side of the goal with the goalkeeper protecting the other side.

2 The player decides to go for goal and to hit an inside foot swerve (see page 18). This will see him strike the right side of the ball with the inside of his right foot to bend the ball to the left.

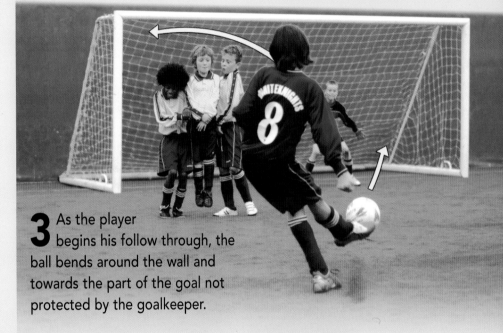

3 As the player begins his follow through, the ball bends around the wall and towards the part of the goal not protected by the goalkeeper.

Penalty

1 This player has placed the ball on the penalty spot and completed her run up. She has decided to hit the ball using an instep drive.

2 She drives through the ball with her instep, looking to keep it on target. If the keeper does not guess and move the right way, then a goal is likely to be scored.

PENALTIES

A penalty is awarded for a serious foul or infringement that occurs inside the penalty area. The ball is placed on the penalty spot and, with only the goalkeeper to beat, it is a fantastic chance to score. Penalties can be hit hard or placed into the corners of the goal using the sidefoot.

GLOSSARY AND RESOURCES

Glossary

assistant referee An official who runs along the sideline and assists the referee during the game.

block tackle Challenging for the ball on the ground using the side of the foot.

cross A kick that sends the ball from the sideline to the centre of the pitch, usually into the penalty area.

cushioning Relaxing and preparing a part of your body to receive and slow down the ball.

deflection When the path of a pass or shot is altered after it hits another player or a goalpost.

dribbling Moving the ball under close control with a series of short kicks or taps.

formation The way a team lines up on the field during a football match in terms of defenders, midfielders and forwards.

free kick A kick awarded by a referee to a team after a foul has been committed. Free kicks can be direct (straight at goal) or indirect (must be passed to a team-mate first).

goal area Also known as the six-yard box, this is the small area around each goal, inside which a goal kick is taken.

hand ball Stopping or controlling the ball with the illegal use of the hand or arm.

instep drive A technique of making longer passes and shots by swinging through the ball and hitting it with the instep of the boot.

jockeying Getting close to a player who has the ball and delaying his or her progress.

marking Moving with and guarding attackers to stop them receiving the ball or from progressing in attack with the ball.

penalty kick A kick taken by a player from the penalty spot close to goal and with only the goalkeeper to beat.

penalty area The large box surrounding each goal inside which a goalkeeper is allowed to handle a ball.

red card A player shown a red card by the referee is sent off and has to leave the pitch, leaving his or her team a player short for the rest of the game.

shielding When a player protects the ball by keeping his or her body between it and an opponent.

sidefoot pass A short, accurate method of passing using the inside of the foot.

through ball A pass sent to a team-mate to get the ball behind defenders.

volley A ball kicked by a player when it has yet to bounce on the ground.

wall A line of defenders standing close together to protect their goal against a free kick.

yellow card Also known as a caution or booking, this sees the referee officially warn a player for a bad foul or other misconduct. Two yellow cards in a single game equal a red card (see above).

Diet and nutrition

Top international football players watch their diet extremely carefully and clubs often employ expert nutritionists to monitor players. Diet is also important at junior and amateur levels.

Eating a good, balanced meal several hours or more before a match gives your body time to get energy from the meal. A balanced diet contains a combination of the three main food groups – carbohydrates, proteins and fats.

Complex carbohydrates are especially good for providing energy for performance. They are found in foods such as pasta, fruit and vegetables. These foods are major features of a professional footballer's diet.

Proteins are important in building muscle strength and stamina. Protein can be found in lean meat, such as chicken, and pulses, such as beans.

www.mypyramid.gov/kids/index.html
Healthy eating is sometimes shown as a food pyramid. This webpage from the US Department of Agriculture provides lots of downloadable files and posters.

www.ehow.com/how_6433_eat-youth-soccer.html
A series of tips for parents and kids on eating a good diet to perform well at football.

Resources

www.bettersoccermorefun.com/dwtext/tablecon.htm
A fascinating website full of skills and drills with the emphasis on playing small-sided games, such as five-a-side, to improve your football abilities.

www.mastersport.co.uk/soccerskills.htm
A large webpage with explanations, drills and tips for a wide range of skills and techniques found in football.

www.jbgoalkeeping.com/
An advanced but exceptionally handy collection of techniques and exercises for budding goalkeepers.

www.asktheref.com/
One of the best sites to visit for more information on the laws of the game, as well as tips for referees.

sports.expertvillage.com/interviews/soccer-basics.htm
An excellent collection of short video clips from football coach, Mick Lewis, showing a range of techniques, from heading to stepovers and dribbling.

www.shekicks.net
Home of the excellent *Fair Game* magazine, devoted to coverage of women's football and with excellent links to women's football websites from all over the world.

soccernet.espn.go.com
Excellent news site with up-to-date information on star players and teams from all over the world.

www.fifa.com
The official website of the *Fédération Internationale de Football Association* – the organisation that runs international football, including the World Cup.

INDEX